GLADINE BRUER

© COPYRIGHT 2024 BY GLADINE BRUER

ISBN: 978-1-963735-91-8

All rights reserved. No part of this book may be reproduced or transmitted in any form or by any means, electronic or mechanical, including photocopying, recording, or by any information storage and retrieval system, without permission in writing from the copyright owner.

The views expressed in this work are solely those of the author and do not necessarily reflect the views of the publisher, and the publisher disclaims any responsibility for them.

To order additional copies of this book, contact:

Proisle Publishing Services LLC
39-67 58th Street, 1st floor
Woodside, NY 11377, USA
Phone: (+1 646-480-0129)
info@proislepublishing.com

This Book is dedicated especially to my great-niece

SKYLAR MADISON HERBERT
JUNE 3, 2014 – APRIL 19, 2020

The First Youngest Known Victim of Covid

5-YEARS OLD

Love Always

Gladine Pannell Bruer

6-2024

P.S.–Also to those who have gone before me

6-2024

Good Mourning

As we go through life, we have happiness, sadness, gladness, tears and smiles. We live for one another and some pass on before us. They're missed in so many ways, some grieve in the hardest of ways — knowing that never again can we sit and talk or look into their eyes and say I LOVE YOU— but for me I have

GOOD MOURNINGS

Deotha Neeley

My first real encounter with life-ending for someone close to me that I can remember is my Great Grandmother.

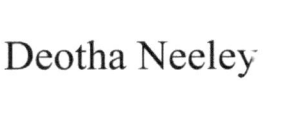

Deotha Neeley

I can and will always remember her glowing face, always a smile and kind words of wisdom to all her children, she fulfilled our every need for growing up and preparing for the world in my times in the late '40s, '50s, '60s and part of the '70s.

A lady of faith, style and dignity — always there for me, no matter what the situation, she uplifted and strengthened my will to move on through life without breaking a stride into what was.

PAWPAW WARREN

My second encounter that I endeavor to remember, and has impacted me, was my Pawpaw Warren's death.

Even though he passed away from Sclerosis because he was an alcoholic but a darn great man/construction worker and carpenter in my lifetime sharing and showing the young men in our family how to be useful and make life comfortable and sure, by making them watch and perform a task that would show them the way — and he knew how to take care and make a living for the family by contributing his gift from God, bestowed upon him while he was on this earth: singing country tunes and plucking on his guitar — dancing and makes me think of another GOOD MOURNING!

Leona Armstead

Granny Nonie, the Grandest Grandma I have ever known—she was firm, tough, straightforward, hardcore on what her beliefs were and she always stood up for them.

There's no crossing her and if you listen to what she had to say you'd better be all ears or you would be in for the lessons of your life.

Nonie was very protective of her family, the advice she gave me I will never forget.

A gentle soul, but like I said hardcore — I always remember her telling me — *Never say anything that you'll be sorry for* — Just keep your mouth shut and keep those negative thoughts to yourself, she would stand by you in thick or thin, have your back at all times, she would make your days and night pleasant and peaceful always from the beginning of her life til the end always

GOOD MOURNING!

The Best Granny Ever
xoxoxo

Maggie Muse Jones

My Great Aunt Maggie, a diva in her own time, a lady who never minced words — made them very plain and to the point, never worried about who would take offense because she was just a straight down the middle of the road lady — no curves, bumps or stops in her road (never in her own lane) traveled in everyone's lane (she couldn't help herself) but a heart of gold — we never had much growing up so Aunt Maggie would make sure we had coats and shoes — she always saved her money and assist wherever needed

She had several husbands (Uncle Muse and Uncle Elmer Jones, two great guys, both were dedicated to her always) of course she outlived both of them — but two Good Men, she always had providers not backsliders.

She made me laugh and taught me how to take care as a young Lady thought of her make for a GOOD MOURNING

JAMES FOSTER PANNEL

My father

Didn't know a lot about my dad but I respected him in my own way— he was busy being a guy in the street and failing all the rules of fatherhood — but still my father — he and my mom couldn't see eye to eye but he was still my father — he was never mean to us— just my Mom, but he is and was my father— he had his faults but that was him.

I really felt a little misinformed after he left us but I will always remember he didn't make me sad, he didn't make me mad. I just know I had a father who never asked for anything — I can remember him always in Good Spirits and me having "GOOD MOURNING"

LONNIE DAVIDSON SR.

The guy of all my growing up years, my uncle— who cherished all of us (his children, nephews, nieces and family)

Uncle Lonnie was my role model for a DAD, his  blueprint is flawless as far as I am concerned.

This man made sure we all were taken care of and always told right from wrong. Polite in his own manner but no nonsense!

He would cook, clean, pray, play, laugh, sing, dance and tell us about ourselves — whether we were right or wrong — you knew his feelings right away/and you know what he would never raise his voice — kept the same tone whatever the situation or mood.

The Male backbone of our Family that I know and will never forget as a "GOOD MOURNING"

CECELIA ALICE BRUER

Mama Alice my Mother-in-Law

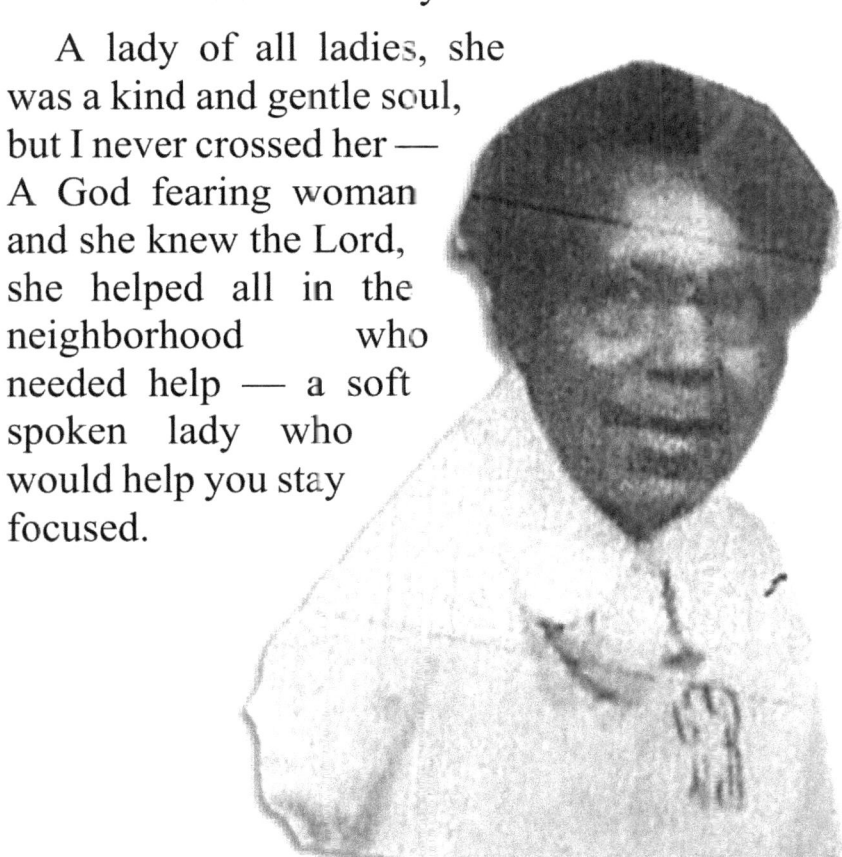

A lady of all ladies, she was a kind and gentle soul, but I never crossed her — A God fearing woman and she knew the Lord, she helped all in the neighborhood who needed help — a soft spoken lady who would help you stay focused.

Remembering her every day and always in the mood for a GOOD MOURNING

PETE BRUER

(Pawpaw Bruer my Father-in-Law)

A man with some rough edges but you could bank on his word, always too truthful—Loved the Ladies and was a good provider.

He treated me as a daughter and showed his sons how to be strong, responsible and true to oneself

No bad or sad thoughts of him, just know as I speak his name or thoughts in passing they are all

"GOOD MOURNING"

ADELE MOSLEY WHITE

My outspoken sister-in-law

You knew where she was coming from the moment she started to speak — No frills, nothing fancy, just herself — always had her siblings' backs and strong-willed about everything!

Her laughter, craziness and directness

No grief just

"GOOD MOURNING"

The FIRM ONE!
xoxoxo

BETTY & BERNARD BROWN

A couple who traveled as one, generous to all and thoughtful always—my sister- and brother-in-law, two kind souls that I will always remember, precious and I will always have for them

"GOOD MOURNING"

My sister and Brother in law of all times
xoxoxo

DEBORAH ANNE MOSLEY

My empathic niece

She had to leave way before her time but she was always selfless, courageous and kind!

She held on to life as long as she could — thinking of her, it's all good — tears were brief, the sadness no more, she will always be in my heart as

GOOD MOURNING

One of my Favorites,
Love you always Deborah Anne
xoxoxo

APRIL DAVIDSON

(My POP-PO)
Gone from our lives in the blink of an eye
Beauty, she had inside and out
I can remember she was just a little sprout
small in statue but big in her heart
a voice like thunder
a smile like the sun
my cousin Pop-po, always no grief just
"GOOD MOURNING"

My Little Cuz/Love
xoxoxo

DEOTHA DAVIDSON PANNELL

(Mama)

My mom — the love of my life, the life that I lived. Thank you, Mother, for everything — I always cherished and honored you!

My mom — my best friend, my role model, my heart, you will never be forgotten.

Without you, I am nothing (was nothing). you always spoke your mind and heart — I'm glad because I always understood you in that fashion — you never disappointed me and I will always be your #1 cheerleader — No matter what — Good heart — Good thoughts — Good vibes always to my Mommy

GOOD MOURNING

My Mama
xoxoxo

Jacquelyn Drewery Bruer

(Jackie)

My sister-in-law — an outspoken young Lady whom I loved like a sister — Funny, straightforward, true to her heart and her family, we had a friendship that was like no other as sisters in laws

She had her funny ideas and so did I, but we never stepped on each other — we respected and honored each other's wishes.

Not a person who would want you to cry once they left this world — just remember the fun stuff and always have a

GOOD Mourning!

My staying in her own lane sister-in-law
xoxoxo

Shirley Brown Armstead

This is a woman of substance, strong beliefs and a pleasant soul! I could always relate to her and we were and will always be bosom buddies

She made me laugh,

She made me cry,

but always in a positive direction and positive thinking.

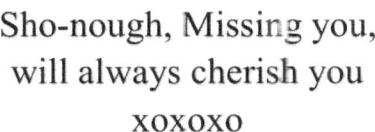

I miss my Aunt Shirley but in a good way

I think of her every day and my hat is off to her because I have nothing but
"Good Mourning"

Sho-nough, Missing you, will always cherish you
xoxoxo

RENA LEE PANNELL

Sister in law

My telephone partner — my energetic bunny

We always laughed and talked good talks, always shared secrets and she loved my Baby Boy Brother (Mr. P.)

A BUSY BEE, there to help anyone who needed help.

Ms. Decorator and problem solver / one of my rock solid partners-in-crime or whatever (*LOL*) we had going on!

None of that sadness going on between us, just

"GOOD MOURNING!"

Miss you, I am smiling—thinking about U
xoxoxo

Wes "Red" Armstead

My younger-than-me uncle —You didn't want to hang around after your wife left, so you eased on out of this crazy world not too soon after her (Aunt Shirley)

I will never forget our weekend visit and the times we spent together as a family (loved every minute).

Will always keep you in my heart and on my mind with

"GOOD MOURNING"

Love, from your Beaner Forever
xoxoxo

EBBIE HERBERT SR.

My personally hand-picked brother-in-law

The kind of guy who was headstrong and dedicated to family—was backup for all stubborn fellows, firm to his beliefs.

A man who lived with my big sister (and that takes a lot *lol*)

My special brother in law
xoxoxo

He loved and cherished her and his family with all his heart.

Adventurous — full of enjoyment with his silly laugh.

I miss you BIG GUY but with

"GOOD MOURNING"

BIG JIM

My brother in law,

a different kind of guy

I can remember him making everyone laugh at family gatherings and being himself

Will always have

GOOD MOURNING

SANDRA SWEENEY EDMONDS

My friend, we enjoyed our younger lives doing things together with our daughters (Pia and Denitra aka Dee)

We were the moms of cheerleaders— group functions or just where ever or whatever we were recruited for — Sand and I — we were RIDE or DIE!

Love and Miss you (Gydene — our inside joke)

Always with a smile on my face / remembering you Sandra Sweeney Edmonds with

"GOOD MOURNING"

Friends Forever
xoxoxo

CARMEN B. GORE

Another loyal and never to be forgotten friend

Carmen, we had worked together and enjoyed lifetime activities together.

She was loyal, true and straightforward — loved her children (Amber & Justin) with all her heart.

Missing your craziness and smile always

GOOD MOURNING

Aunt Della Pannell Milner

This is my hardcore unpredictable Aunt whom I have shared many memorable times with.

She was a person to reckon with at times, but deep down inside she was a good person, we shared visits, trips and situations together and her heart was in the right place most of the time —

she will always be one of my favorites, with thoughts of peace

GOOD MOURNING

SKYLAR MADISON HERBERT

The Beautiful baby girl that's on the cover of this book

GOOD MOURNING

This young lady, my Great niece Skylar Madison Herbert, I really didn't get a chance to know her like I wanted to: one of the reasons is that she lived in another State (Michigan) but I got the reports on her from her Grandmother Herbert (Leona Pannell Herbert, my Big Sister)

Skylar was and still is and always will be her Grandma' Herbert's (Apple of her eye) – Skylar, a diva in her own right and a huge ray of sunshine for our family — Quick to learn and show others the way.

Her parents: Ebbie and LaVondria Herbert, their Baby girl setting the world on fire with her positive and outgoing attitude, giving up her FIVE years here on earth for a cause (COVID—Skylar being the first child to be exposed to the horrible germ-plagued our children in the United States of America)

Skylar will always be a GOOD MOURNING TO ALL IN THIS COUNTRY

Love you Skylar, Always
    xoxoxo

Incredible memories inspiring me—reflecting on happy moments. Searching every nook and cranny of time on earth with these awesome persons has made me realize—physical absence is the only lonesome feeling I have in remembrance of them!

My mind wonders in order to spend precious time with them and feel great and smile with such satisfaction, knowing I will always have such a fulfilling and complete thoughts and never grieve for them without soul laughter and high spirits— just like when I could physically see, touch, hug, and shed happy tears at all the great times we spent together.

Whether we were on the phone— reuniting at family gatherings or just in passing— Good Mourning!

Help us to Heal, Focus, Reminisce, Cherish moments, Honor and Reflect on remembering and understanding with NO REGRETS!

Do you remember your first responds when you are given the message of the passing of our family or friends? Was it the feeling of

- DENIAL
- HEARTBROKEN
- SAD
- ANGRY
- NUMB

After gathering your thoughts and finding comfort with the message, be at peace with the healing and acceptance that you have shared so much with that person that you know

It's going to be Okay!

NO QUESTIONS about Why?

When we all know nothing is forever.

Emotions running wild and regrets have NONE

Accept they are no longer physically with you and you will miss them, but remembering all that living and sharing life's lesson you enjoyed with them helps to ease away the message you have just received.

Changing your perspective of death to a GOOD MOURNING knowing you have not been betrayed or left out because they equipped you with all the laughter, smiles, and thankful moments.

Memories stay with the LOVE.

Keeping the faith of GOOD MOURNING!

TODAY

Today is today and we are in it.

Tomorrow, a maybe, my dear friend

So smile and thank God for the day of light

Because the day after tomorrow might not be

in sight!

Dedicated to All who can appreciate Today
With a Smile
Gladine Pannell Bruer

www.ingramcontent.com/pod-product-compliance
Lightning Source LLC
LaVergne TN
LVHW050027080526
838202LV00069B/6954